My First Animal Library
Meerkats
by Penelope S. Nelson

Bullfrog
Books

Ideas for Parents and Teachers

Bullfrog Books let children practice reading informational text at the earliest reading levels. Repetition, familiar words, and photo labels support early readers.

Before Reading

- Discuss the cover photo. What does it tell them?

- Look at the picture glossary together. Read and discuss the words.

Read the Book

- "Walk" through the book and look at the photos. Let the child ask questions. Point out the photo labels.

- Read the book to the child, or have him or her read independently.

After Reading

- Prompt the child to think more. Ask: Have you heard about meerkats before reading this book? What more would you like to learn about them after reading it?

Bullfrog Books are published by Jump!
5357 Penn Avenue South
Minneapolis, MN 55419
www.jumplibrary.com

Library of Congress Cataloging-in-Publication Data

Names: Nelson, Penelope, 1994– author.
Title: Meerkats / by Penelope S. Nelson.
Description: Bullfrog books edition.
Minneapolis, MN : Jump!, Inc., [2020]
Series: My first animal library
Audience: Age 5–8. | Audience: K to Grade 3.
Includes bibliographical references and index.
Identifiers: LCCN 2018039322 (print)
LCCN 2018040672 (ebook)
ISBN 9781641285599 (ebook)
ISBN 9781641285582 (hardcover : alk. paper)
Subjects: LCSH: Meerkat—Juvenile literature.
Classification: LCC QL737.C235 (ebook)
LCC QL737.C235 N45 2020 (print)
DDC 599.74/2—dc23
LC record available at https://lccn.loc.gov/2018039322

Editor: Jenna Trnka
Designer: Jenna Casura

Photo Credits: AekaPhoto/Shutterstock, cover; CraigRJD/iStock, 1, 6; Rosa Jay/Shutterstock, 3; neotemlpars/Shutterstock, 4, 23tl, 23tr; R. Maximiliane/Shutterstock, 5; Nachaliti/Shutterstock, 7, 23bl; Sylvain Cordier/Getty, 8; DragNika/Shutterstock, 8–9; Sally Wallis/Shutterstock, 10–11; anetapics/Shutterstock, 12–13, 23tm; Klein & Hubert/Nature Picture Library, 14–15; designbase/iStock, 15; TommL/iStock, 16–17; Namthip Muanthongthae/Shutterstock, 18; NHPA/SuperStock, 19, 23bm; Steffen Schellhorn/Age Fotostock, 20–21; Farinosa/iStock, 22; Africa Studio/Shutterstock, 23br; cparrphotos/Shutterstock, 24.

Printed in the United States of America at Corporate Graphics in North Mankato, Minnesota.

Table of Contents

Meerkats Watch 4

Parts of a Meerkat 22

Picture Glossary 23

Index 24

To Learn More 24

Meerkats Watch

A meerkat peeks out of its burrow.

It looks for danger.

It is safe to leave.

Time to find food!

One keeps watch.

hyena ·····▶

What does
it watch for?

Predators.

Like hyenas.
Or large birds.

They dig for bugs.
What else do they eat?
Snakes. Scorpions.

scorpion

roots

They eat roots, too.

Why?

It is dry where
they live.

They get water
from roots.

Their group is called a mob.

How many are in it?

Up to 25!

mob

The mob stays together.
Why?
To stay safe.
They fight off snakes!

They rest in the afternoon.

Why?

The sun is hot.

The burrow is cooler.

Pups stay in the burrow.

pup

18

They leave the burrow.

Mom teaches them.

They find their own food.

Parts of a Meerkat

eyes
Meerkats have dark fur around their eyes. This helps protect their eyes from the sun.

nose
Meerkats have an excellent sense of smell for finding food.

ears
Meerkats have excellent hearing to listen for danger.

snout
Pointed snouts help meerkats eat food from the small holes they dig.

claws
Claws help meerkats dig to find food.

legs
Meerkats have short legs and can stand on their hind legs while keeping watch.

Picture Glossary

burrow
Holes or tunnels in the ground where animals live.

mob
A group of meerkats.

peeks
Looks at something secretly or quickly.

predators
Animals that hunt other animals for food.

pups
Young meerkats.

roots
Parts of plants that grow underground and get water and food from the soil.

Index

burrow 4, 16, 18, 20

dig 8

eat 8, 11

food 5, 20

mob 12, 15

peeks 4

predators 7

pups 18

rest 16

roots 11

watch 6, 7

water 11

To Learn More

Finding more information is as easy as 1, 2, 3.

❶ Go to www.factsurfer.com

❷ Enter "meerkats" into the search box.

❸ Click the "Surf" button to see a list of websites.